To your Bro.

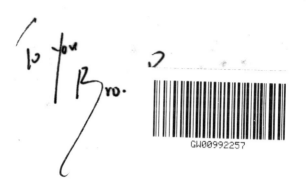

GW00992257

Six Lies the Devil Uses to Destroy Marriages

The Lord is Lord and He is A Covenant Keeping God.

by
Lisa Comes

Be encouraged in your walk of faith for Everything. He is a Rewarder!

Lakewood Church
P.O. Box 23297
Houston, TX 77228

ISBN 0-912631-98-8

Contents

Husbands, love your wives, even as Christ also loved the church, and gave himself for it; that he might sanctify and cleanse it with the washing of water by the word, that he might present it to himself a glorious church, not having spot, or wrinkle, or any such thing; but that it should be holy and without blemish. So ought men to love their wives as their own bodies. He that loveth his wife loveth himself. For no man ever yet hated his own flesh; but nourisheth and cherisheth it, even as the Lord the church: for we are members of his body, of his flesh, and of his bones. For this cause shall a man leave his father and mother, and shall be joined unto his wife, and they two shall be one flesh. This is a great mystery: but I speak concerning Christ and the church. Nevertheless let every one of you in particular so love his wife even as himself; and the wife see that she reverence her husband.

— Ephesians 5:25-33

Introduction

What is the will of God for your marriage?

Simply stated, God wants you to love your mate, and He wants your mate to love you.

He wants you to leave your mother and father, to cleave unto your mate, to nourish, to cherish, to admire, and to respect him or her as the Word of God says.

Three things you must know about marriage
1. God wants you to have a happy marriage

God wants you to be happy in your marriage. He wants the two of you, husband and wife, to be one. The Bible says that you are one flesh. He wants you to be in agreement, at peace with one another. God wants you to have a strong, consistent, stable, and beautiful marriage.

You may feel that your marital situation is far from God's plan for the ideal marriage. Probably most couples fall short of having the marriage relationship they'd like to have. But I believe you can get there. It is not impossible to have what God wants you to have. The Bible says in Ephesians 1:3 that God wants to bless us with all blessings. And a marriage is to be blessed.

So the first thing I want you to know and fully understand is that God wants to bless you in your marriage relationship. He wants you to have a beautiful, happy marriage.

2. God has a plan for your marriage

The second thing you must understand is that God has a plan for your marriage. He has a specific purpose for your marriage — a reason for you and your mate to be together. The two of you together have a specific place and ministry in the Body of Christ.

I think often about the marriage and ministry of my mother and father. Where would I be, where would my family be, where would this ministry be if they had let the devil destroy their marriage? Certainly they wouldn't be reaching and blessing other people. They wouldn't be happy in their own lives. But they are fulfilling God's plan for their marriage . . . and for their ministry. The two are interrelated — tied up together. You must realize that God has a plan for *your* marriage — *your* ministry together. I don't necessarily mean that you're called to a full-time ministry, but God does have a ministry for you. He's called *every* believer to be a minister for Him.

Remember, God established the home before He ever established the Church. And until our homes come together, until our marriages come together, the Church is always going to be hurting. The Bible says "Two are better than one . . . for if they fall, one will lift up his companion'' (see Ecclesiastes 4:9,10). God wants you and your mate to take your place in the Body of Christ and fulfill the plans He has for you.

3. Satan is the enemy of your marriage

The third thing I want to establish with you is that you have an enemy. Satan is your enemy! And he doesn't want your marriage to be happy. He doesn't want God's perfect will to be fulfilled in your life. He'll do everything in his power to thwart the plan of God in your life. So we're going to talk about the schemes and tactics the devil uses to destroy marriages. It's important to learn to recognize his schemes, his plans, and his lies in order to prevent him from destroying your marriage.

I have learned in working with people and their marriages over the past few years that the devil doesn't have any new plans and schemes. He uses the same old lines over and over. People come to me and say, ''My mate said this, that, and the other.'' Or they'll say, ''You know, I have this thought, and this temptation.'' I can almost tell them what they're going to say before they say it because I hear the same thing over and over again.

How foolish the devil is! He has no new tricks. He deceives the Body of Christ with his same old lies again and again. We must learn to detect the voice of the evil one when he whispers these lies in our ears. If we don't, we'll let him deceive us and destroy our marriages.

In this book we're going to take a look at the most common deceptions Satan uses against marriages. You'll learn to recognize and refute from God's Word the six lies the devil most often uses to destroy marriages.

The Bible says in John 8:44 that the devil is a liar and the father of all lies. The devil lied to Adam and Eve in the very beginning and he's lied to God's people ever since. Unfortunately, too often when couples hear these lies, they believe them. They accept Satan's deception as reality. I want you to learn to recognize truth and realize when the enemy is whispering in your ear.

Perhaps you are not troubled with all of Satan's lies — some of the things we'll talk about may not apply to you. But look at them all. Then if you ever get in a place where you're struggling and you hear one of these lies, you'll be able to recognize the devil's work right away and be able drive the enemy away from your marriage.

Satan's First Lie: God's Word Doesn't Provide Healing for Marriages

The first lie the devil tells so many hurting couples — Lie One — is simply, "God's Word really doesn't provide marriage healing."

I hear this so much — "I just don't think God can heal my marriage. I don't see in the Bible where He healed marriages. I just don't think it's in God's Word."

How sad when people really believe they have no choice except to suffer in a bad marital situation or else get a divorce. Well, that's just not true. That's a lie of the devil! God doesn't want you to suffer and He doesn't want you to get a divorce. He wants to heal your marriage.

Matthew 19:5 and Mark 10:9 both say the same thing — *What God hath joined together let no man put asunder*. First Corinthians 7:27 says if you are married, do not seek a divorce. Then, in Malachi 2:16, God said, "I hate divorce."

Now, surely even reason and logic tell us that if God says not to divorce then He must have provided a

11

way to prevent it. And He has! Marriage healing is a part of the whole plan of redemption. Underscore that sentence! Get it into your spirit! *Marriage healing is a part of the whole plan of redemption.*

We are redeemed from divorce

Jesus redeemed us on the cross. He redeemed us from sin, sickness, and disease. The Bible says He restored all that the devil took from us and that includes a blessed and beautiful marriage. According to Galatians 3:13,14 Jesus redeemed us from the curse of the law. And let me tell you, marriage problems are a curse of the law. Deuteronomy 28 makes it clear that it's a curse to live in divorce and adultery. It talks about being away from your family and being away from your home — that certainly can describe the effect of divorce and adultery. And it's a curse. The Bible says Jesus redeemed us from that curse. So we don't have to live with divorce in our lives.

One day the Pharisees came to Jesus and said, "Well, Moses permitted the people to divorce." And this was Jesus' answer: "But from the beginning this was not so" (see Mark 10).

What He was saying was that this was not God's original plan, not His will. So Jesus, on the cross, brought us back to the beginning. He brought us back to His original plan, and that is for you to have a blessed and beautiful marriage. You don't have to stay in an unhappy marriage and suffer. And you don't have to get a divorce. You can be free. Your marriage can be healed.

Jesus is a Healer. We all know that. That's one of His greatest characteristics — He is a Healer. He heals

12

bodies. He heals spirits. He heals minds. He heals relationships. And He heals marriages. Jesus wants to heal *your* marriage.

Don't settle for second best. Don't settle for less than God's perfect will. Marriage healing is a part of redemption.

It's never too late for God

I know a young couple who went through a really traumatic marriage tragedy. They were even Christians, active in church and the work of the ministry. But the devil began to attack their marriage. The husband became discouraged and drifted into sin. He slipped into worldly practices. One thing led to another. Finally, he got involved in adultery. He left home. In spite of his actions, his wife didn't want a divorce. But he divorced her anyway. So this wife thought, *Well, I'll just go on with my life. I'll try to be happy. I'll do something for God.* She was thinking about going to Bible school, traveling and doing things for the Lord. And God saw her heart.

She thought it was too late — it was all over. The devil told her there was nothing in God's Word that pertained to her situation. She didn't know there was healing for her marriage — wrecked by divorce.

One day as she was sitting in Lakewood Church listening to a speaker, God dealt with her heart and said, "My thoughts are higher than your thoughts. You don't have to lose your husband and your marriage." Then He spoke to her and said, "I want to restore your marriage!"

Remember, this is after they had already divorced. From that day on she began to seek God.

About one year later, God got hold of this husband right before he married someone else and brought him home. What a miraculous healing took place! Today this couple is reunited and working together for the Lord. They have a blessed and beautiful marriage.

But the point I want to make is that at first the wife really didn't know God's Word provides healing for broken marriages. The devil lied to her. But as soon as she knew the truth she grabbed hold of it and believed God to restore her home.

There is hope for you

There are so many hurting people today. They don't know how much God cares about their marriage. They don't know what God's Word has to say. They just know that they are desperate. They need help.

Perhaps you feel this way – you're discouraged and in despair. I want you to know that God does want to heal your marriage. If God *can* heal one marriage, He *can* heal all marriages. If God *will* heal one marriage, He *will* heal all marriages. He wants to bring you and your mate together no matter how bad the situation looks. He's a Healer. Don't ever accept the lie of the devil that God's Word is silent on your marital needs. God does heal marriages.

Satan's Second Lie:
You Need to Start All Over —
New Partner, New Marriage

The second lie the devil uses to destroy marriages sounds so believable that many are deceived by it. I often hear individuals and couples repeating this vicious falsehood. The devil whispers, "You've made such a mess of your marriage that there's no hope for it. You should start all over. You need a brand-new marriage and a brand-new partner."

Has the devil ever suggested this to you? Has this thought come to you as you've agonized over your problems? It may appear to be logical at first, but you must recognize that it is a lie of the devil.

I've had people say to me, "You just don't know the mess I'm in. If you knew all my problems you wouldn't say that I'd have to stay in my marriage." People get so hurt, so tormented that they don't see any possible way out. The only solution they can imagine is the last resort of divorce. I feel such compassion for them — they're so broken in their hearts. And God loves those precious wives and husbands just as they are . . . just where they are. But they just don't understand that God wants to heal their present marriage and that divorce and a new marriage is not the answer.

God wants the best for you

We serve a loving God who knows and wants what is the best for His children. And if divorce was His best, if a new marriage was the best thing for His children, I believe with all my heart He not only would allow, but would encourage divorce. But He doesn't. So I have to believe that God knows more than we do, and He is not for divorce.

John 4 tells the story of Jesus meeting the Samaritan woman at the well. During His conversation with her, a woman He had never seen before, Jesus told her, "You've been married five times and the man you're living with is not your husband." That revelation helped the woman recognize that Jesus was a prophet.

One day as I was meditating on this scripture passage, the Lord impressed me that this woman's story proved that starting over again with a new marriage and a new partner wasn't the answer. She apparently thought marriage was her problem because she'd tried five different times and still wasn't happy. Then the Lord spoke to me, "She needed an encounter with the Lord Jesus Christ — the Savior of her life. She needed an encounter with the One who would save her marriage."

You don't need another partner. You don't need another marriage. What you need is an encounter with the Lord Jesus Christ — the Savior and Healer of all marriages. Do you see that? Marriage will continue to fail for you until you learn to overcome and make

16

changes in your life. Marriage cannot succeed for you until you learn to obey the Word of God.

The spirit of divorce

Divorce is a spirit. Hear me, now. Divorce is a spiritual force of destruction, and that spirit will follow you around all of your life until you learn to take authority over it.

Statistics show that the divorce rate is much higher in second and third marriages. A fresh start with a new partner just isn't the answer. The problem is that you're under attack by spiritual forces — principalities and powers sent by the devil to destroy your marriage. You're involved in spiritual warfare.

So many times people have said to me, "Lisa, I thought this marriage would be different. I thought this mate would be better. I just knew this husband was going to be better than my last one. I was sure this marriage was going to be better. But it seems like we have more problems than ever."

God knows what is best for you. If you don't learn to overcome and drive out that spirit of divorce, it will follow you around all of your life.

I'm not trying to make you feel condemned if you are in your second or third marriage now. Just learn that you have missed it! God looks at you as a learner and not as a failure. You are responsible to obey the knowledge you have now. He's saying to you, "Now you know! Now you have the Word of God. Obey it. Make this marriage work."

One reason second and third marriages fail even more frequently than first marriages is that people take their hurts, problems, and faults with them when they re-marry. They get married again, thinking, "This marriage will get me out of my bad situation. This will rescue me out of my problems." Too often they fail to realize that their new spouse has many problems and hurts, too. Many times he or she has been married before. So their new marriage starts off with lots of extra scars and wounds. The pressure keeps building up and eventually there is an explosion.

God knows what is best for us. He wants us to be happy in our first marriage. A divorce is not the answer. Another marriage is not the answer. He wants you to be happy now.

"Creative divorce" isn't the answer

Newsweek magazine, in the August 24, 1987 issue, printed an article titled, "How To Stay Married — The Divorce Rate Drops as Couples Try Harder to Stay Together." The article described several different couples and their efforts to work out their marital problems. One statement in the report really struck me because of the way it confirms the Word of God — it just shows that even the world is admitting that what God's Word says is true. Here's what it said: "The period of creative divorce we went through is going out of style," says Donald Wertlieb, associate professor of the Eliot Pearson Department of Child Study at Tufts University. "The suffering for grownups and children is phenomenal."

Satan will tell you that starting over is your only answer — that divorce is really just a fresh start. But that's a lie. Even the world's experts are recognizing that throwaway marriages aren't the answer — "creative divorce" isn't the answer. Another marriage is not the answer.

God will help you

What is the answer? The Word of God! God's Word tells us how to solve our marriage problems. God created marriage. He knows how to make it work.

We need to go to the Creator of marriages and say, "God, how can we get out of this mess? How can we work out these problems? How can we have a beautiful marriage?" If you'll do that, God will help you. He can and He will!

Humble yourself before the Lord and say, "God, I want to please You. I want to do Your will. I don't like the situation I'm in but I want to please You. Help me have a beautiful marriage."

God will answer your prayer. He will begin to speak to you. And He'll show you what you can do to solve your problems. He'll get you out of your miserable situation if you will cooperate with Him.

Satan's Third Lie: You Married Out of God's Will

The devil tells many people, "You made a mistake. You should never have gotten married. Your marriage is not blessed because you married out of the will of God."

That is a lie! Whether you were a believer or not, or whether or not your mate was a Christian, God was a witness between you and your mate at your wedding day. The vows the two of you made were done before God.

Malachi 2:14-16 teaches that the marriage ceremony is solemn and sacred to God and, in His eyes, you have a covenant relationship with your mate and with Him. God says you are to guard yourself so that you will not break faith with your partner. You are not to break that covenant, that relationship. You and your mate are one flesh in the eyes of God.

The circumstances surrounding your marriage may not have been pleasing to God. You may even have disobeyed Him. But that doesn't mean that your marriage is cursed. When you got married, you entered into a holy and sacred covenant. The person you married became right for you. That partner became yours forever. And you are to guard yourself and your spirit so that you will not break faith.

Don't let the devil lie to you. God can make something beautiful out of your mistakes and failures. He can make blessings out of curses. He can remake the shattered broken pieces of your marriage into a vessel of honor, stronger and more beautiful than you ever hoped for! Protect what God has given you. Protect your wife. Protect your husband. Protect your children. Don't let the devil have what God has given to you.

A "mistaken" marriage?

I know a wonderful couple who almost certainly made a tremendous mistake in getting married. They were religious people but they really didn't have a personal relationship with Jesus. They didn't know Him as their Lord and Savior. The wife said she knew she was making a mistake when she got married, but she did it anyway. The husband was drunk on their wedding day and she practically had to drag him to the wedding. About four years later when they had two children and another one on the way, he left. He became an alcoholic, got into adultery, and moved clear across the country from his wife. He said he didn't ever want to see her again.

Even though this young woman really didn't know Jesus, she realized that in getting married she had made a vow and a covenant before God. She knew that she had made a lasting, binding decision. So she said, "I'm going to stick it out."

22

During the traumatic, crushing months that followed, she cried out to God for help, and the Lord Jesus revealed himself to her. She accepted Him as her Savior. Then she began to pray for her husband — faithfully, patiently, in faith, believing. After one-and-a-half years of separation, God brought him back home to her! You've never seen a more beautiful marriage than they share today. He is saved and they're both Spirit-filled and completely involved in the work of the Lord. God is using them to help bring healing to marriages.

Now, let me ask you — Who is to say this couple's marriage was a mistake now? Who is to say she made a mistake in holding on when he wronged her and left her? Don't you think God was working way back then? God's will was to bless them even when she was saying, "Oh, we've made a mistake. We've blown it. But I'm going to stick to it."

Today, no one thinks this couple made a mistake in marrying. People notice that they seem to be made for one another. And the same thing is true for you. No matter what anyone says, you do have the right mate. You have found Mr. Right, Mrs. Right. Your marriage is in God's will. So don't believe the devil's lie. You stick with your marriage partner and protect what God has given you.

Satan's Fourth Lie: You've Been Hurt Too Much To Love Again

When your heart is broken and you feel your mate has hurt you too deeply for words to express, the devil loves to whisper in your ear. He says, "Your mate has hurt you and wronged you too much. How could you love him or her anymore? You could never love like you used to so you might as well split up."

I refer to this often because I've personally been healed of a broken heart. I know what it's like to have hurt, rejection, and grief in my spirit. The devil came to me when I was really down and said, "You can't ever love that person anymore. He's hurt you too much. You might as well just give up." And that lie nearly destroyed me.

The Bible says that heartache crushes the spirit and that a weak and broken spirit cannot sustain a person (see Proverbs 15:13; 18:10). So it's hard for a person in this state to love — or have hope of ever feeling love again.

But God has the answer for this, too. You don't have to live with a broken heart and a wounded spirit.

You don't have to live with rejection in your heart. You can be completely free — right now, this minute — you can be free of that hurt. And when you get free, you will see that love is still there inside your heart. You'll discover that you really can love as God loves. God replaces your limited, imperfect love with a supernatural love when you let Him heal your broken heart.

What Jesus did for you

The Bible teaches that Jesus not only bore our sins and sicknesses on the cross, but listen to this — *He bore our griefs*. See if you relate to these things: He bore our weaknesses. He bore our sorrows. He bore our pain. He bore our distresses. And the Bible says that He felt rejected on the cross. He didn't do that for himself — He did it all for you. He bore all of that pain and all that sorrow so you wouldn't have to live with it.

Luke 4:18 and Psalm 147:3 tell us that Jesus heals the brokenhearted and binds up their wounds. Those verses are directed to you. Where the Spirit of the Lord is there is liberty — there is healing and peace. And the Spirit of the Lord is near you right now to heal and restore you and set you free.

I encourage you to release all the anger and unforgiveness you may feel — all malice and all bitterness that you may have in your heart. Decide to release that — turn it loose and let it go. God wants to set you free from the hurt of rejection. You don't have to live with that sick feeling anymore.

I could tell you many wonderful stories of how God has healed broken hearts. A woman came to Lakewood Church who had been separated from her husband for several months. They had endured great strife because of serious communication problems. She reached the point where she had no love for her husband. When she left him, she ended up backsliding into the world. She gave up on her husband, on God, on her marriage, and on herself.

Then one night she found herself at Lakewood Church. There she heard me talk about how God could heal a broken heart instantly. She believed God's Word and asked for prayer. Immediately God removed the hurt and put a deep love in her heart for her husband. She said she felt like a new person. Later she went to talk with her husband and they both gave their lives totally to Jesus. Today they have a beautiful marriage.

This is what God can do for you. You see, the love of God has been shed abroad in your heart by the Holy Ghost (see Romans 5:5). But you must not allow that love to be buried by hurts and wounds. Let God heal the hurts and uncover that love in your heart.

Healing for a broken heart

There was a time in my life when I was so hurt and wounded. I felt sick in my spirit. So I told the Lord, "God, I cannot live with a broken heart. I cannot walk in faith and do Your will with this sick feeling. You have to set me free of this rejection."

I was so oppressed, so down that I couldn't see the way out. But when I cried out to God, He healed me instantly. He cleansed my wounds and removed the scars. I am free to walk in the fulness of God's blessings.

You may say, "That sounds so simple." It is! We make things too hard sometimes. We think we have to go through some great drawn-out, protracted inner healing process. But that's not the way it is. The healing of a broken heart is a part of redemption and we need to receive it just like we receive salvation or physical healing. You can receive healing of a broken heart instantly if you will just cry out to God right now.

Satan's Fifth Lie:
Your Marriage Has to End
in the Case of Adultery

Is there hope for your marriage if your mate has committed adultery? Can you be expected to forgive? Can the unfaithful partner, who has repented, receive forgiveness and be restored to his family? When one marriage partner gets into adultery, the devil loves to go to the offended mate and say, "Well, your marriage is over. There's nothing that can be done. You could never forgive your mate. It will never be the same." But, the devil is a liar.

Many people get sidetracked from the will of God when it comes to adultery. Certainly it is a terrible thing. But let me tell you something — adultery is not too big of a problem for God. No matter what bondage you or your mate may be in, God can set you free. He can bring healing and reconciliation if you allow Him to.

In Old Testament times, the penalty for adultery was death. What a severe punishment! But when Jesus came, He said, "I've come with a new law. I've come with a law of love."

One day they brought a woman to Jesus who had been caught in the very act of adultery and asked what should be done to her. They probably expected Jesus to say to her, "That's it — forget it! It's the end of her life. Stone her."

Did Jesus do that? Remember, He is our Example. No, the Lord gazed at that accusing mob and said, "Let the one who is without sin cast the first stone." One by one they backed away. Then Jesus tenderly said to the adulteress, "Woman, your sins are forgiven. Go and sin no more."

Be like Jesus — forgive!

That's how Jesus reacted to adultery. And if Jesus can do it, we can do it. He's given us the same power — the power of the Holy Ghost — to forgive the same way He forgives, to love like He loves. Just because your mate has been unfaithful to you doesn't mean your marriage is over. Don't ever let the devil tell you that. Your marriage is not over. God can heal your hurt. God can help you forgive.

As my dad, Pastor John Osteen, often says, "Only the guilty need mercy." We must remember the times when we needed mercy, when we blew it, and how God forgave us and gave us another chance.

Maybe your husband or wife had to give you a second chance — or a third or fourth chance — for some offense or failure. You have to remember that. We never have a right to hold unforgiveness in our hearts. When you forgive, a healing takes place in your heart. If you will just make the decision to obey the Word of God and say, "Yes, God, I will forgive," then the Lord will bring love back into your heart. He will restore your love and give you the power to forgive and forget even an offense as serious as adultery.

First things first

So often a woman or man has come to me personally, and said, "My mate has committed adultery and I'm so hurt I don't think I want him/her back anymore. I don't even know why I'm here. I want help, but I just don't think I want my mate back."

I always tell these people, "Don't worry about your marriage now. Let's take care of you. Let God do a work in you."

As I minister to these individuals, I help them see that God can help them release all unforgiveness and hurt so they can be free. After they allow God to heal their hurts, it never fails that they come back and say, "I think I want my marriage restored. I do love my mate after all."

What changed their mind? We didn't talk them into it. They allowed God's healing power to heal their hurts. And when that happens — change occurs.

Adultery is not an unforgiveable sin

Something takes place in the hearts of people who forgive and obey the Word of God. And when those people we prayed with decided to forgive, when they decided to release their anger and bitterness and let God heal their broken hearts, then God did a work in *their* lives. Then they could see that they could forgive their mates and go on together — even after adultery. So don't ever let the devil tell you that your marriage is over because your mate or you (or both of you) have committed adultery. Adultery is not an unforgivable sin. Jesus forgives and He is the Healer.

Satan's Sixth Lie:
My Mate Is a Sinful Unbeliever
Who Will Never Change
So Our Marriage Could Never
Be Blessed by God

So many times I've had individuals tell me that they'd decided they might as well get a divorce because their spouse was not a Christian. "My mate is an unbeliever, living in deep sin. He is never going to accept Jesus! There's no chance he'll ever live for God. So our relationship is doomed because we're 'unequally yoked.' There's no hope. We could never have the blessed marriage that God wants His children to have."

I gently remind those who tell me this that God loves their mate just as much as He loves them. And I also tell them that salvation is not just for them, but for their whole family. Psalm 68:6 says that God sets the solitary in families. He puts the lonely into the warmth and security of a loving home. And I believe He saves that one person in order to bring a whole family into the Kingdom of God.

God saved you and got His message to you for a

reason. He has drawn you by His Spirit. Acts 16:31 says, *Believe in the Lord Jesus Christ, and you will be saved, you **and your household*** (Revised Standard Version, emphasis mine).

I believe that it is ordained of God for you to be reading this book. You didn't receive this information just by chance. I believe this with all my heart! God has drawn you by His Spirit. And He brought you and me together through this book for a reason — to let you know that He wants to heal your marriage, save your mate, and give you a brand-new life.

You're probably familiar with 2 Corinthians 10:3-5 which talks about the weapons of our warfare. The Living Bible's rendering of this passage, in verse 5, says that *you are to grab rebels and bring them back to God through prayer*. Isn't that good? You can grab your mate through prayer and bring them back to God.

Second Peter 3:9 says, *God is not willing that any man perish, but that all come to repentance.* That word "all" *includes your mate!*

Joel 2:28 says, *In the last days I will pour out my spirit on all flesh.* Does that exclude your mate? No, of course not. God is pouring out His Spirit on your mate! You can't manipulate or change your mate in your own power. I must stress this. But when you pray, God changes people. He changes things. He changes circumstances. He rearranges events in order to see people come into the Kingdom of God. He will use His full power in order to see your marriage healed. He will work if you pray.

Can God change a person's will?

Saul of Tarsus was one of the most wicked men alive in Bible days. He persecuted Christians. He stood at the feet of those who stoned Stephen, one of the first martyrs for the faith. Before he died, Stephen said, "Lord, I pray that You won't lay this charge against these people." Stephen prayed for his murderers, including Saul.

Later, Saul was on his way to Damascus, with papers granting him authority to persecute more Christians and put them in jail. Now, I believe the Church, the Body of Christ, was praying for Saul at that time. No doubt, in the natural, they'd have been happy to see him dead. They'd have been relieved to see this persecutor out of the scene. Someone may have even said, "How could somebody like Saul ever come to know Jesus? It could never happen! God is just going to have to remove him from this earth in order to free us from his wickedness." But I believe those early Christians, like Stephen, were praying for Saul.

God knew what it would take to get Saul's attention. On the way to Damascus, suddenly a bright light shined on Saul and the Bible says he fell off of his horse. He found himself blinded — and he couldn't see for three days. Then Saul was ready to listen! He had changed his mind. God brought him to the place where he had a change of heart. If we will trust in God and His ways, He will bring your mate to the place where his/her heart can be changed, too.

Are you or your mate a Jonah?

Think about Jonah. God spoke to this prophet to go to Ninevah and preach repentance. Jonah didn't want to go, so he got on a ship sailing in the opposite direction. The Bible tells us he caused havoc in that boat because he was running from God. The sailors were fearful and anxious to know why they were having such awful problems — they were about to sink! They were in such a terrible storm, they had to throw their cargo overboard to lighten the ship. Then they realized that someone on board was the source of their problem. They cast lots to determine who it was and found out that Jonah was the culprit. They said, ''Jonah, you've got to get away from us or we're all going to die.'' So they threw him overboard.

You know the story, how God had a fish swallow him up. And inside the belly of that fish Jonah decided to listen to God. He changed his mind. He repented and began to sing praises unto God. God knows exactly what to do to bring people around — we just need to trust in Him.

God knows how to get your mate's attention. As you pray, God will draw them by His Spirit. He knows how to change his or her mind. So don't ever let the devil tell you that your spouse is too far away from God to ever change because nothing is too difficult for Him.

Pray and Let God Restore Your Marriage

Your marriage and family are worth saving. They are worth the sacrifice, the all-out effort, the investment of all your resources to save. So don't give up. Don't accept the devil's lies that you're better off to get a divorce.

The first and best thing you can do to rebuild and restore your marriage is to PRAY.

Pray for your home.

Pray for your mate.

Pray with faith.

Pray with boldness.

Pray with persistence.

You must come against the devil who is influencing your mate. Remember, you don't have power over your mate, but you do have power over the devil. Pray and take authority over the spirits that are driving your mate away from God.

Don't preach to your mate. Often this only antagonizes and irritates. Instead, live a godly life before your mate. Refuse to give up, even if it seems to be taking too much time. Give God time to act.

Let me suggest two scriptures you can use in praying over your mate. Second Timothy 2:26 talks about delivering people that Satan has snared and held captive. Second Corinthians 4:3-6 tells how Satan has blinded the minds of many who need to see the glorious light of the Gospel of Jesus Christ. You can apply these scriptures as you pray for your mate, that he or she will come to their senses. The devil takes people captive to do his will, but you can demand of him to release your mate in the Name of Jesus.

If you pray, if you are persistent, I believe your mate will come to know the Lord. You can have a blessed and beautiful marriage.

Let God do the changing

This same principle also works and applies to couples who may not be facing divorce, but do have room for improvement. You may not be pleased with all that your mate is doing. There may be things that are wrong in your mate's life and you've tried to call them to his or her attention, but your words seem to fall on deaf ears. Quit nagging and start praying! Pray that God will touch your mate's heart. If you pray, God will do the changing. Don't try to change your mate by yourself. Let God do it. You do what you know to do. The change begins in you. You make the changes you need to make in yourself. Then start praying that God will work on your mate.

Remember, God's will is for your marriage to be blessed. God has a perfect plan for your marriage and the devil is trying to thwart that plan. But I believe you are going to detect Satan's lies, his plans, and his schemes, and you're going to drive him out of your life.

Let's pray together: *"Father, I thank You that on the cross Jesus bore all of our rejection. He bore all of our hurts, our wounds, and our pain. So right now we claim the healing provided in the atonement and ask You to do a work in this life. Father, I thank You that You are doing surgery in this spirit to remove the anger and bitterness! I thank You for healing this broken heart and for binding up these wounds, in the Name of Jesus.*

"Now, devil, I command you to take your hands off this friend. You'll not torment them any longer in the Name of Jesus. You will not torment them with hurtful memories. Set this dear one free in the Name of Jesus.

"Now, Father, I ask that You will give this person a supernatural love for their mate in the Name of Jesus. I pray that this love will begin to rise up and get deeper and greater every day. Give this friend the vision You want them to have. Let them see themself and their mate together — happily married, serving You, Father. Put that vision into this heart, even now. Oh, Father, I thank You for working out every situation and every little detail of this marital situation.

"Thank You for delivering both of these marriage partners! Thank You for showing us how to pray, and showing us how to love, in Jesus' Name. Thank You for the power of the Holy Ghost to help us forgive in Jesus' name. Amen."

A Prayer For My Marriage

Father, in the Name of Jesus, I come boldly to Your throne of grace to find help and mercy in this time of need. I come with Your Word, Father, concerning my marriage. The Bible says in 1 John 5:14-15, This is the assurance we have in approaching God: that if we ask anything according to His will, He hears us. And if we know that He hears us — whatever we ask — we know that we have what we asked of Him.

I know Father, that it is Your will for my marriage to be healed. I know that Your will is for my mate and I to be in agreement, to be at peace, and to have a beautiful relationship. Therefore, I have confidence that You will heal my marriage. I thank You, Father, that You were a witness on our wedding day when we made our marriage vows. I confess that my mate and I will guard ourselves in our spirits so that we will not break faith with one another (see Malachi 2:14,15).

I praise You, Father, that my mate and I are no longer two, but we are one flesh. You have joined us together. And what God has joined together, no man will separate (see Mark 10:7,9). I know that Satan has come to destroy my marriage. But I also know that Jesus came to bring life to my marriage (see John 10:10.)

I thank You, Father, that You have given me power over all the power of the enemy (see Luke 10:19). I know that my mate is not my enemy. My fight is against the principalities and powers of darkness (see Ephesians 6:10-12). In the Name of Jesus, I resist the devil and he must flee from me and my mate (see James 4:7). I take authority over the spirit of confusion, strife, adultery, and divorce and all the powers of darkness that have come to destroy my marriage. In the Name of Jesus, we are free from the power of the devil.

Father, I pray that You will show me the changes that I need to make. I pray as David prayed, I desire truth in my inner being; make me therefore to know wisdom in my inmost heart (see Psalm 51:6). I desire to know the truth because the truth will set me free. Help me, Father, to walk in love toward my mate.

Now I know, Father, that You are not willing that my mate perish, but that they will come to repentance (see 2 Peter 3:9). I pray that You will enlighten the eyes of my mate's understanding in order that they may know the hope to which You have called them. I thank You, Father, that my mate will turn to You and we will serve You all the days of our lives. I thank You, Father, that my mate and I cling to one another and we love each other as Christ loves the church (see Ephesians 6:22-32). I pray that we will get rid of all bitterness and anger and that we will be kind and compassionate to one another, forgiving one another just as Christ forgave us (see Ephesians 4:31,32).

I know, Father, that You have a specific plan and purpose for me and my mate together. And I thank You for perfecting that which concerns me (see Psalm 138:8). Amen.

Note: You may wish to insert the name of your marriage partner in the appropriate places in this prayer to make it more personal to you.

Never, Never Live Up

We are more than Conquerors through God.

Jehovah - Shammah!

Bro. Edward.

BOOKS BY JOHN OSTEEN

*Miracle For Your Marriage
*A Place Called There
*ABC's of Faith
*Believing God For Your Loved Ones
 Deception! Recognizing True and False Ministries
 Four Principles in Receiving From God
*Healed of Cancer by Dodie Osteen
*How To Claim the Benefits of the Will
*How To Demonstrate Satan's Defeat
 How To Flow in the Super Supernatural
 How To Minister Healing to the Sick
*How To Receive Life Eternal
 How To Release the Power of God
 Keep What God Gives
*Love & Marriage
 Overcoming Hindrances To Receiving the Baptism in the Holy Spirit
*Overcoming Opposition: How To Succeed in Doing the Will of God
  by Lisa Comes
*Pulling Down Strongholds
*Receive the Holy Spirit
 Reigning in Life as a King
 Rivers of Living Water
 Saturday's Coming
 Seven Facts About Prevailing Prayer
 Seven Qualities of a Man of Faith
*Six Lies the Devil Uses To Destroy Marriages by Lisa Comes
 Spiritual Food For Victorious Living
*The Believer's #1 Need
 The Bible Way to Spiritual Power
 The Confessions of a Baptist Preacher
*The Divine Flow
*The 6th Sense...Faith
 The Truth Shall Set You Free
*There Is a Miracle in Your Mouth
 This Awakening Generation
 Unraveling the Mystery of the Blood Covenant
*What To Do When Nothing Seems To Work
*What To Do When the Tempter Comes
 You Can Change Your Destiny

*Also available in Spanish.

Please write for a complete list of prices in the John Osteen Library.
Lakewood Church • P.O. Box 23297 • Houston, Texas 77228